GLACIER BAY

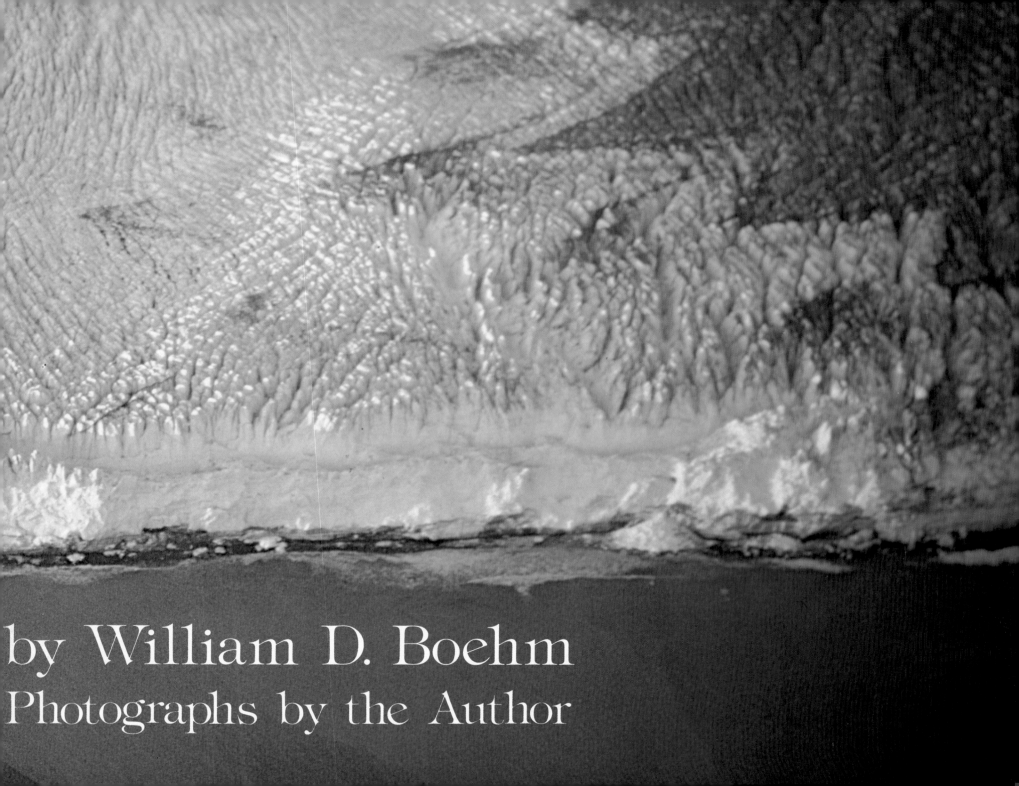

by William D. Boehm
Photographs by the Author

Designed by Roselyn Pape

Library of Congress Cataloging in Publication Data
Boehm, William D
    Glacier Bay: old ice, new land.
    1. Glacier Bay National Monument. I. Title.
F912.G5B57   917.98'2   75-17886
ISBN 0-88240-056-8

ALASKA NORTHWEST PUBLISHING COMPANY
Anchorage, Alaska 99509

About the author: William Boehm took the photographs for this book during a summer spent at Glacier Bay working for the National Park Service. He lived in an old cannery shack on the west shore of Dundas Bay and traveled throughout the Glacier Bay region from there. Boehm has degrees in both forestry and wildlife biology; he lives in Seattle and works for the King County Public Health Department.

Contents

The Cover—Hair seals at the foot of the glacier in Muir Inlet. Seals are not intimidated by the big ice walls, and bask happily on the ice beneath.
Pages 1 and 4—Plateau Glacier at Wachusett Inlet.
Pages 2 and 3—La Perouse confronts the Pacific.

Introduction

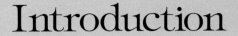

In geological time two centuries is an eye-blink, yet it was less than two centuries ago when Vancouver's Expedition, which had discovered and thoroughly explored Puget Sound 2 years before, sailed past Glacier Bay, Alaska, without knowing it was there. All they saw was a gigantic wall of ice at the edge of the sea.

The ice was in retreat at the time, but the fallback had begun recently, perhaps within that century. The only hint to what lay beneath the glacier was a small inlet, just another dent in a rugged coastline.

The late 1700's climaxed an age of exploration and discovery along the upper coasts of the continent carried on by several nations. Then, having probed the most promising bays and straits without finding the fabled Northwest Passage, their interest lagged. Several decades passed before anyone noticed that Icy Strait's northside shoreline had developed a new bay that the early explorers had missed.

Sunset on the outer coast at La Perouse Glacier; fog on the mountains at Dundas Bay's north arm. The front slopes of the Fairweather Range capture abundant precipitation (most of it snow) to feed extensive glacial systems on the mountains' flanks.

(*NOTE: A large, shaded-relief map of Glacier Bay National Monument is provided at the back. A map showing principal features appears on page 31.*)

By the late 19th century the phenomenon in progress had excited many scientists. Records, including photographs, have been kept ever since. Glacier Bay has been the jackpot not only for those who study glaciers but for botanists, biologists, climatologists and geologists.

It is as though nature had provided a time-lapse motion picture, in which frames exposed hours apart are projected at normal speed to let us see the seed sprout and the plant force its way up through the soil, blossom and produce fruit in a matter of minutes. Geological time has been condensed in Glacier Bay, with massive glaciers enacting in a century what took milleniums to do during the ice ages.

Geologists have not had to depend entirely on detective work such as digging to uncover a moraine to examine ancient glacial striation. They can study photographs taken over a period of 85 years of peaks emerging from the shrinking ice fields, and read firsthand accounts written by their immediate predecessors.

The cycle of plant life has been speeded up, too—from lichens to climax forests within the four generations of specialists who have been on the scene to record the process. Within a human lifetime new streams are formed and biologists can determine how long it takes for fish to become established in the waters. Birds and mammals move in on newly exposed land, a natural process that has been witnessed personally over the years by those who have used Glacier Bay as their laboratory.

Two centuries ago the ice over Glacier Bay was at least 4,000 feet deep. Thus the geologists have been afforded a scale model of the massive fronts that advanced and retreated in past milleniums.

Muir Inlet, the northern branch of Glacier Bay, at breakup.

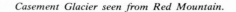
Casement Glacier seen from Red Mountain.

There has been much speculation, for example, about ocean levels that rose or fell, depending upon how much water was locked up in the icecaps. A countermovement to a rising sea level, though, is a rising land surface as the weight of the ice is removed from the earth's pliant crust.

Ice 4,000 feet thick would exert a pressure of more than 3 million tons a square mile. At one point the ice is now back 65 miles from the front Captain Vancouver observed, taking quite a load off the earth's crust.

Observations and measurements for more than eight decades have given geologists the unique opportunity of watching the land rise. Around the Beardslee Islands, in the entrance to Glacier Bay, the rise has been 4 centimeters a year, or a foot in slightly more than 8 years.

There are other bonuses for the scientists. On the outer coast of the Monument are pocket areas that were not engulfed in the most recent ice advance and date back to the previous ice age, providing contrasts for study. Melting glaciers also have exposed the remains of mature forests of the past.

And then, just to keep everybody guessing and intent, not all the glaciers are receding. Several are creeping, even surging, forward. Among them is Grand Pacific, which had retreated very fast, clear back to the Canadian border. Its turnabout misled some Canadians who in 1974 incorrectly assumed that British Columbia had gained a new outlet to the sea. (See "Out of Bounds," page 30.)

This then is the importance and excitement of Glacier Bay National Monument. Understanding it, visitors share in the excitement even if they visit only to sightsee.

—*The Editors*

Geological History

Opposite—*Johns Hopkins Glacier, one of the growing, or advancing, glaciers.* Below—*Gulls feeding at Point Corolus.* Bottom—*Goose Cove, on the east shore of upper Muir Inlet (Bruce Barton).*

Glacier Bay National Monument contains some of the most beautiful and biologically rich wilderness in Southeastern Alaska. It is a place where ice-covered peaks rear above crinkled fjords that probe deeply into mountain ranges, a magnificent blend of sea and land.

A broad spectrum of habitats exists within the 4,381-square-mile refuge: an outer coast of rocky cliffs and sandy beaches populated by brown bear and pierced by glaciers that project into the open Pacific; spectacular deepwater fjords teeming with seals, whales and screaming flocks of puffins and gulls; gentle, timbered lowlands; islands; sheltered coves; and, higher up, luxuriant alpine meadows.

North arm of Dundas Bay.

Taylor Bay.

Situated just above the Alexander Archipelago of Southeastern Alaska, about 70 miles northwest of Juneau, Glacier Bay is part of a large glacial basin almost surrounded by mountain ranges. The highest, the Fairweather Range, is the birthplace of a large number of tidewater glaciers. Bordering the northern and eastern boundaries of the Monument is a group of smaller peaks that feeds the extensive glacial systems of the upper sections of the Monument. The gentle rivers that meander through the forests of Bartlett Cove spring to life off the southern slopes.

The southern portion of the Monument, including the lower reaches of Dundas and Taylor bays, is split by an extensive fjord system that penetrates northward. Access is by boat or floatplane.

Glacier Bay is a changing scene of physical forces. Located in an active seismic zone that extends across the

north Pacific rim, Glacier Bay has been the site of both geologic stresses and climatic swings. Originally the land mass that now makes up the Monument was submerged, covered by salt water. Extensive marine sedimentation occurred in this period. The land mass, responding to earth forces, was alternately raised above and dropped below sea level over a long period of time, resulting in a series of marine and nonmarine deposits.

An interval of mountain-building followed in which marine sediments were lifted well above sea level.

Igneous activity at the same time metamorphosed some of the older beds of marine strata, creating extensive beds of slates and schists, and creating large granite batholiths and basaltic intrusions.

Erosion and alteration of the physical features of the bay followed in the form of glaciation. A cooling trend caused

Opposite—*Glacial history on the rock at Hugh Miller Inlet.*

Left—*Terminal moraine at Melbern Glacier.*
Below—*The arch at Fern Harbor is on the edge of the National Monument but accessible to visitors.*

the accumulation of ice and snow at higher elevations, forming extensive ice fields throughout Southeastern Alaska as well as the rest of North America. This happened during mid-Miocene to early Pleistocene epochs, 20 to 1 million years ago.

Pleistocene glaciation was intense in Southeastern Alaska, as evidenced by the area's glacial valleys and vast moraines. Extensive glacial deposits are located at places distant from present glacial sources—for example the extensive forest-covered moraines on the outer coast of the Monument.

The last extensive ice encroachment to influence Southeastern Alaska was approximately 10,000 years ago. Much of the area was covered by ice that, on retreat, left deposits of compact till (silt, sand, clay and gravel sediments) throughout the region. These more recent deposits can be distinguished from those left by previous glacial advances by studying soil samples in the laboratory or by field investigation of stratification.

Certain areas west of the Fairweather and Saint Elias ranges were not covered by the last ice advance and, in these areas, plant and animal communities continued to develop unimpaired by climatic change.

About 7,500 years ago a warming trend caused some of the glaciers in Glacier Bay, such as Brady and those of the outer coast, to shrink to about their present sizes. Then parts of the Muir, Wachusett and Adams inlets were repopulated by hemlock forests that flourished for several thousand years.

A new ice advance, around 4,000 years ago, covered the forests and, for a long period, preserved them in a deep freeze. The retreat of the main body of ice from Glacier Bay a century ago uncovered the debris layer and the remains of trees. Stumps of this ancient forest jut from the bared moraines of Adams and Muir inlets.

The massive ice field in Glacier Bay had started to dissipate several hundred years ago. The large glacial

Opposite—*The ice field southwest of Melbern Glacier (which is north of Grand Pacific in Canada).*

20

terminus reported by explorers in 1794 indicated that recession was in progress. During the following century, the ice front retreated northward toward its source. By 1860 it had wasted back to a position near the mouth of Muir Inlet.

The western trunk of the glacier continued to recede for another century until it stabilized at what is now called the Grand Pacific Glacier, 65 miles from the mouth of the bay. After a period it started to move forward again. Since 1949 it has advanced nearly a mile.

The northern trunk, of which the glaciers of Muir and Wachusett inlets are remnants, is still retreating. The ice terminus of Muir has been receding at an average rate of a quarter mile per year, although it has retreated as much as 5 miles in 7 years. Trim lines indicating the past thickness and the quarrying action of Muir Glacier are evident along the flanks of Mount Wright and the ridges adjacent to McBride and Riggs glaciers.

By losing its vast ice sheet with its tremendous weight, the lower parts of Glacier Bay are experiencing glacial rebound. New subtidal rocks and small islands are slowly appearing, and existing islands, such as the Beardslee Islands, are experiencing an uplift of 4 centimeters per year. How far the land will rise as the elastic properties of bedrock slowly recover before an equilibrium can be established is not known.

In contrast to a general pattern of retreat, some of the area's tidewater glaciers are experiencing some growth and they are advancing. The Johns Hopkins and Grand Pacific are examples of growing glaciers.

Present glacial waterfalls at Point Dundas, and the signs of ancient glaciers elsewhere. The interstadial tree stump is at Wolf Point, the scoured rock at Charpentier Inlet.

Glaciers

The conditions that determine the advance or retreat of a glacial system at any time are complex. Glaciers are a product of climate and are dependent upon favorable meteorological conditions—temperature and precipitation—to nourish and sustain them.

Colder temperatures in the Pleistocene epoch caused the creation of a system of ice fields far more extensive than exist today. Precipitation fell as snow over large areas of mountainous terrain and sustained the growth of extensive glacial systems throughout Southeastern Alaska.

Temperatures favorable for snow accumulation are now common only to the higher elevations of its mountain ranges where very little melting takes place. Given a large surface for accumulation and plentiful precipitation, the snowpack seasonally increases in thickness. The enormous mountains of ice shown here were formed by this process.

Above—Ice in Muir Inlet; harbor seals at left.

Opposite—McBride Glacier.
Overleaf—The Brady Icefield; ice in the foreground
flows toward Hugh Miller Glacier.

Clouds on the Fairweather Range feed the glacial system.

This build-up that sustains a glacial system is especially apparent in the Fairweather Range of the Monument's outer coast. The mountain barrier removes great amounts of moisture from shore-bound storms that originate in the North Pacific. The result is precipitation of up to 180 inches a year, most of which falls in the form of snow during the winter months. The extensive glacial systems thereby sustained on the flanks of this range include the Brady Icefield, the largest ice accumulation in the Monument.

Other factors that can influence the health of a glacial system are surface winds, radiation (which influences melting), cloud cover, reflectivity and the physical properties of the ice itself. An accumulation of rock and dirt on the glacier may alter melting rates.

Most glaciers have an accumulation zone at an elevation where snowfall exceeds the amount of seasonal melting and a wastage area where melting exceeds accumulation. The two areas are separated by the snow line evident during summer.

Snowfall on the accumulation area becomes compressed into ice, adding to the mass of ice already present. Gravity causes the mass to flow slowly downhill, spilling over into areas of least resistance. Rock and debris under the glacier's tremendous weight carve great U-shaped valleys and fjords out of the bedrock.

Storm clouds over Icy Strait.

Previous page—The face of Riggs Glacier in Muir Inlet.

Opposite—The glacier has carved a valley out of rock as one might carve a bowl out of wood. This is the south tongue of Geikie, which flows toward the Dundas River.

28

OUT OF BOUNDS

A glacier that retreats a mile a year and continues to do so for 75 or more years might be considered predictable. *Predictable* is, however, the wrong word to apply to a glacier, as Canadian author-photographer Richard Harrington found out.

Harrington knew that Grand Pacific Glacier had been receding toward Canada for years. Confident that its terminus had crossed the boundary and gone out of the Monument, he and some friends sought to acknowledge the event by planting the Canadian flag on British Columbia's "new seaport." Harrington's article and a photograph of the event appeared in *ALASKA* ® magazine, January 1975.

By the April issue, the glacier and the international boundary had been put back where they belong with the following correspondence:

Photos reprinted from *ALASKA* ® magazine

Comparison of the photo taken in September 1965 with the photo taken in August 1974 clearly shows that Grand Pacific Glacier is advancing into Alaska rather than retreating into the Yukon. A study of the photos also shows progress in the eventual linkup of Grand Pacific Glacier with Margerie Glacier. (USGS photo by Austin Post)

"Last summer I carried out geologic field research in Tarr Inlet from early July through the end of August. After reading Harrington's article, I find several glaring errors that must be corrected.

"It is true that from about 1925 through 1948 British Columbia would have had access to sea water at the head of Tarr Inlet. During those years, the tidal terminus of Grand Pacific Glacier had retreated back into the Province of British Columbia. By 1954, the terminus of Grand Pacific Glacier had advanced out of Canada and was back in the United States once again inside Glacier Bay National Monument. By the late 1960's, it was well inside the national monument....

"The International Boundary is not where Mr. Harrington would like it to be, but runs in a direct northeasterly bearing from Boundary Peak Number 161, Mount Forde, whose elevation is 6,880, across Grand Pacific Glacier to the summit of Mount Barnard, elevation 8,124, which is Boundary Peak Number 160. Thus at this time one would have to walk northward up the Grand Pacific Glacier about one-half mile before he would reach the boundary between Alaska and British

Columbia.... In 1954 Grand Pacific's terminus was right at the International Line and it has been advancing slowly ever since....

"If Margerie and Grand Pacific (glaciers) continue their advance they should unite by 1980."

—*Dr. George M. Haselton*
Clemson, South Carolina

Harrington says, "I went by the government survey done by a Mr. Forde on the spot in 1926, and 1964 reports by Whitehorse enthusiasts. Subsequent satellite photographs seem to indicate that the glacier now extends about a mile into Alaska."

Dr. William O. Field of the American Geographical Society, an authority on the glaciers near Tarr Inlet, commented on the incident: "At the end of July 1974, the terminus (Grand Pacific Glacier) was between 1,950 and 2,000 feet from the station. Thus at this point, the terminus was from 4,000 to 4,050 feet over the boundary into Alaska. To the west, the terminus roughly paralleled the boundary and at the west end was perhaps as much as

4,500 feet from the boundary. I do not believe there was any exposed water surface in Tarr Inlet closer than 4,000 feet to the boundary."

Below—"It appears that we planted the Maple Leaf in the wrong country," wrote author Richard Harrington after his article "New Port For Yukon?—Beachhead on Tarr Inlet" drew protests from both American and Canadian experts on the area. Believed to be in Canada at the time of the helicopter party's visit to Tarr Inlet in the summer of 1974, the flag-supporting cairn is actually more than a mile inside Alaska. (Richard Harrington)

1965

Linkup with Margerie Glacier.

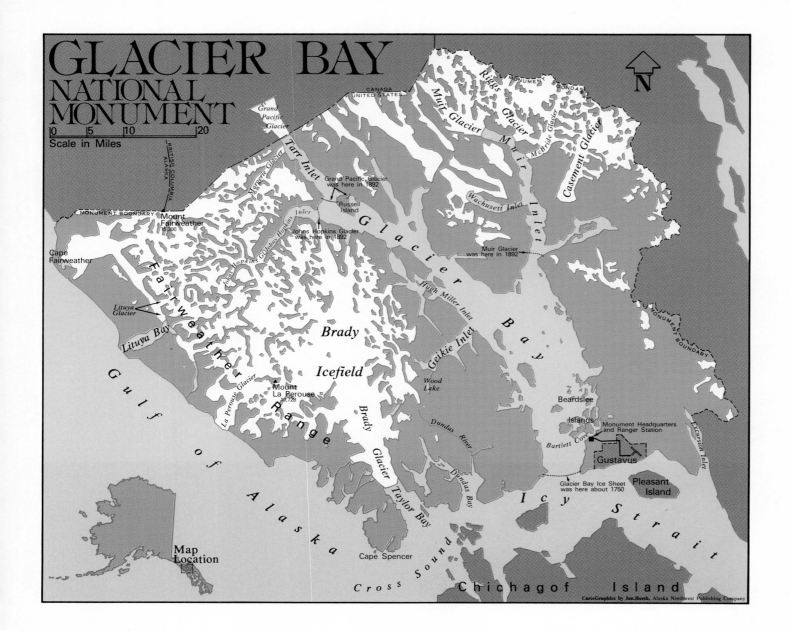

GLACIER BAY
NATIONAL MONUMENT

0   5   10   20
Scale in Miles

N

Grand Pacific Glacier

Riggs Glacier

Muir Glacier

McBride Glacier

Casement Glacier

CANADA
UNITED STATES

BRITISH COLUMBIA
ALASKA

Margerie Glacier

Tarr Inlet

Grand Pacific Glacier
was here in 1892

Russell Island

Wachusett Inlet

Muir Inlet

MONUMENT BOUNDARY

Mount Fairweather
15,300

Inlet

Johns Hopkins Glacier
was here in 1892

Cape Fairweather

Johns Hopkins G.

Johns Hopkins Inlet

Muir Glacier
was here in 1892

Glacier

MONUMENT BOUNDARY

Fairweather

Hugh Miller Inlet

Lituya Glacier

Brady

Bay

Lituya Bay

Icefield

Geikie Inlet

La Perouse Glacier

Mount La Perouse
10,728

Wood Lake

Range

Beardslee

Brady

Islands

Monument Headquarters
and Ranger Station

Gulf

Dundas River

Bartlett Cove

Excursion Inlet

Glacier Taylor Bay

of

Dundas Bay

Gustavus

Glacier Bay Ice Sheet
was here about 1750

Pleasant Island

Alaska

Icy   Strait

Map Location

Cape Spencer

Cross   Sound

Chichagof   Island

CartoGraphics by Jon.Hersh. Alaska Northwest Publishing Company

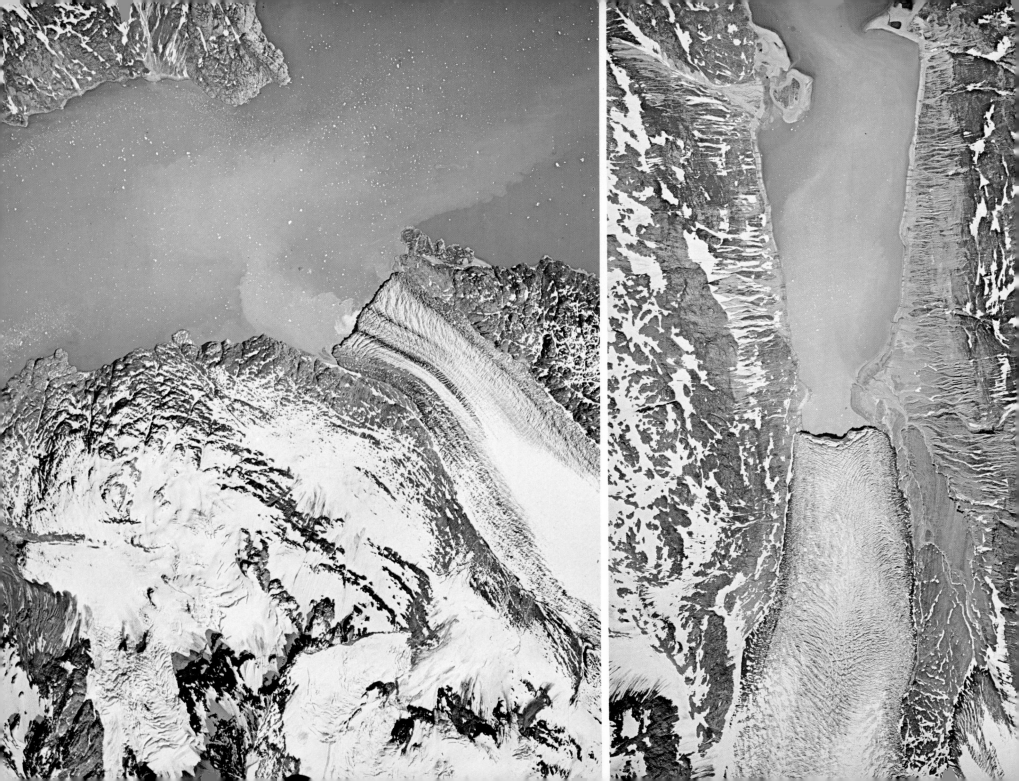

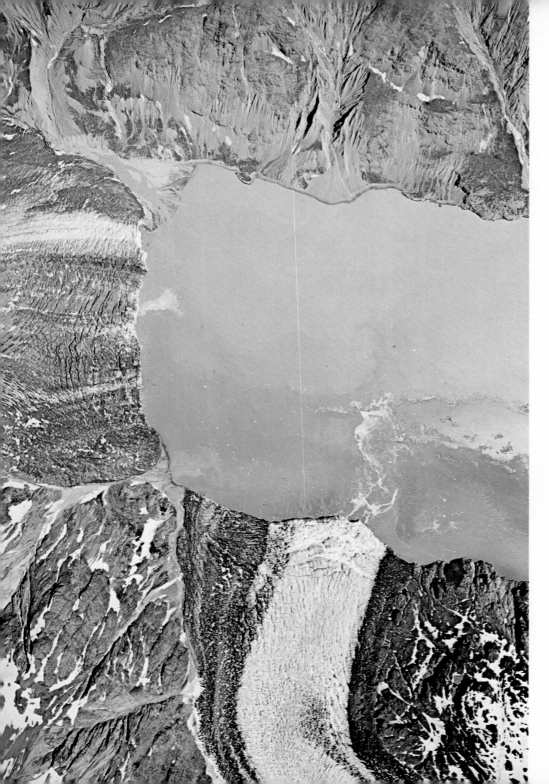

Left—*Lamplugh Glacier carries ribbons of silt into the entrance of Johns Hopkins Inlet.* Middle—*Reid Glacier, emerging from the bottom of photo, crumbling into an arm of Glacier Bay.* Right—*Margerie Glacier, bottom; the face of Grand Pacific Glacier is partially visible in upper left* (U.S. Geological Survey).

In Glacier Bay, an impressive example of glaciation is Muir Inlet. The Muir Glacier carved through its bedrock base to a depth of about 4,000 feet, 1,700 feet of which is now below sea level. The quarrying and abrasive action of the glacier shows on the rock that forms the sides of the inlet. A barren trim line indicates the glacier's height before recession a century ago, and great horizontal striations just above tidewater are witness to the tremendous grinding and polishing forces at work below.

Where complete melting of a glacier mass equals its forward movement, a terminus develops. On land the glacier deposits all the debris, gravel and quarried rock picked up during its downhill movement in a terminal moraine. Rocks weighing several tons may fall out of the glacier, but the greatest volume deposited is made up of the silt, sand, clay and gravel mixture known as till.

By contrast, stagnating glaciers develop moraines that are moderately level and marked by ponds and standing areas

33

of black ice. The lower Casement Glacier area of Adams Inlet is an example of a stagnating glacier.

The continual forces at work in glacial movement are seen throughout the Monument. Approaching a tidewater terminus by boat, one hears the groaning, grinding and popping of the ice mass as it moves over bedrock. As the glacier moves forward, the ice face is made unstable by salt water that melts the glacier's foundation, and pieces of ice up to 200 feet high and weighing several tons crack off the face and thunder into the bay.

Glacial movement takes many forms, but always there is evidence of movement. Left—Muir Inlet. Middle left—Casement Glacier. Middle right—Margerie Glacier, from snow peak to water.

Above—*The ice flow from Muir Glacier spills into Muir Inlet.*

A Brief Geography

Left—Mount Crillon, elevation 12,726 feet, one of the highest peaks of the Fairweather Range. Center—Orville and Wilbur. The two peaks on the skyline were named for the Wright brothers in 1961. Mount Orville, on the left, has an elevation of 10,495 feet; Wilbur, 10,820 feet, is a mile to the west. Looking west, Johns Hopkins Inlet in the foreground. Right—Mount Fairweather, elevation 15,300 feet, seen from Melbern Glacier.

Glacier Bay National Monument lies within a large, horseshoe-shaped rim of mountain ranges that reach their maximum elevation in the Fairweather peaks in the western part of the Monument. Highest mountains in the range are Mount Fairweather, 15,300 feet; Mount Lituya, 11,750; Mount Crillon, 12,726; and Mount La Perouse, 10,728. The 30-mile-long Brady Icefield, the largest ice mass in the Monument, lies at the foot of these peaks along their eastern slopes.

West of the Fairweathers, muskeg and richly timbered slopes face the Pacific and are split by the La Perouse and Fairweather glaciers that penetrate to the sandy beaches.

The outer coast of the Monument extends from Cape Spencer to several miles beyond Cape Fairweather. Since

Above—*The new green thicket at Taylor Bay contrasts with the dense forest of maturing spruce at Bartlett Cove. Right—Muir Inlet. Wachusett Inlet in background. looking west from Red Mountain.*

Above—*A view over Berg Bay.* Left—*The flanks of North Marble Island; a waterfall at Dundas Bay.*

this part of the Alaska coast, as far north as Yakutat and beyond, escaped Pleistocene and more recent glacial advances, a mature rain forest and muskeg complex developed. Along the sandy beach edge, gnarled and twisted Sitka spruce and hemlock grope for existence and seek to survive high onshore Pacific winds. Mats of lichens cling to the trees and give the forest a special character.

Deep in the forest, western hemlock, spruce and Alaska yellow cedar grow in dense stands, shutting off the sound of surf, creating a stillness broken by the splash of a waterfall or a raven's call.

At the head of Lituya Bay, north along the Monument's west coast, a network of glaciers tumbles down to salt water. Crillon, Lituya and Cascade glaciers add special elements to the steep forested slopes and ice-covered mountains of the jewellike bay. Tlingit Indian legend says that Kah Lituya, a monster of the deep waters, has bear sentinels watching for intruders that may come into his bay. If the domain is

Overleaf—*Dixon Point, on the outer coast.*

39

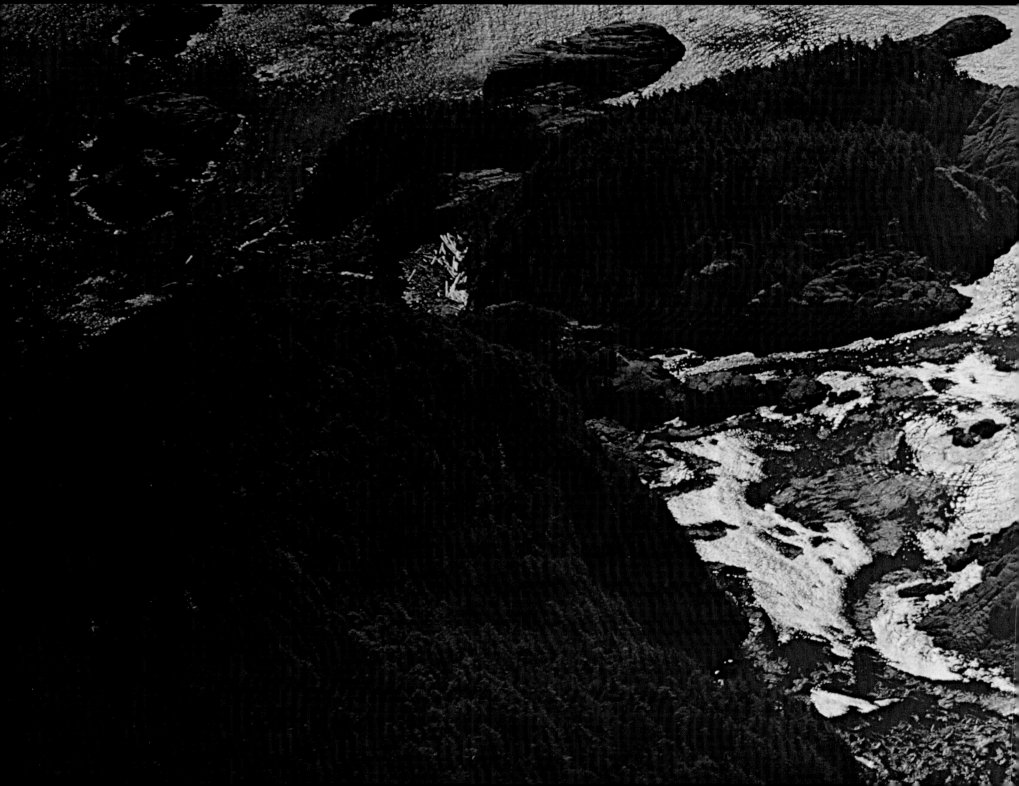

invaded, Kah Lituya and his sentinels shake the water, causing tidal waves that drown the intruders.

This was the Tlingit answer to the tidal waves that have occurred in the bay for centuries; the most recent followed a 1958 earthquake. At that time, millions of tons of rock were dislodged from the mountains into the headwaters of the bay, touching off a 100-foot tidal wave.

Cape Fairweather, at the northwest corner of the Monument, is the terminus of Fairweather Glacier. The stagnated ice front supports a crown of spruce forest that has taken root in several feet of gravel on top of a thick layer of black ice. The ice melts at different rates on the glacier's pitted surface, creating small depressions and hummocks. Spruce trees growing there tip their crowns to all points of the compass.

The northern boundary of the Monument is bordered by the Takhinsha Mountains, a range that averages 6,000 to 7,000 feet in elevation. Mount Harris, at 6,575 feet, is the source of the Muir, Riggs, McBride and Casement glaciers, all of which may be seen from Muir Inlet.

The moderate peaks of the Chilkat Range, up to 5,000 feet high, mark the eastern edge of the Monument. Featuring timbered slopes of spruce and hemlock on the lower elevations, the Chilkats' alpine meadows and snowfields provide the water source for the Beartrack and Bartlett rivers and the streams of Adams Inlet.

Excursion Inlet on the Southeastern corner of the Monument has heavily timbered shores. It contains a large cannery, located on leased Forest Service land, that processes much of the salmon caught locally by commercial fishermen.

The southern shore of the Monument parallels the interlocking waterways Icy Strait and Cross Sound, and it is as heavily vegetated as the outer coast. There are several bays along the strait, such as Dundas Bay, which is ringed by a wilderness of spruce and hemlock forests and flowered

Opposite—Mount Crillon stands over Lituya Bay at 12,726 feet; the mountain is about 10 miles east of the bay. Above, clockwise—*Riggs, Casement, and McBride glaciers at Muir Inlet.*

Above—*The Brady Icefield west of Glacier Bay extends about 18 miles from north to south and is 10 miles wide.* Right—*Fog and mist are common on Dundas and Taylor bays. The southern shoreline of the Monument, along Icy Strait, is as heavily vegetated as the outer coast.*

44

Left—*Taylor Bay's shoreline has many unusual rocky cliffs dotted with caves. The flowers and ice were seen along Muir Inlet.* Above—*Fast tides at the mouth of Glacier Bay can make boating hazardous.*

meadows on a broad alluvial plain. By contrast, Taylor Bay, the other major bay in the area, is more exposed to storms off the Pacific. Its shoreline has rocky cliffs dotted with caves and the Brady Icefield spills out just short of tidewater at its head, creating an extensive alluvial plain that slopes to salt water.

Glacier Bay, the body of water that bisects the Monument, has two major branches: Muir Inlet to the north and Tarr Inlet on the northwest. These major fjords join Glacier Bay near its midpoint, where it is about 10 miles across. South of this point gentle forested slopes make up much of the shoreline and islands dot the bay. The islands are ringed by extensive marshes and tide flats that, in season, host large numbers of ducks and geese.

The bay narrows at its mouth to about 4 miles. In this area small boat operation is often hazardous; tides of 5 to 7 knots are frequent.

This moss-covered chunk of rock at the edge of Dundas Bay is the home of a spruce tree, determined to exist at the spot where it rooted.

History

Complex Indian cultures were well established along the coast of Southeastern Alaska long before Bering's voyage of discovery in 1741. Tlingit Indians lived in the vicinity of Glacier Bay and closely resembled their southern neighbors, the Haidas, as well as the Tsimshian, Nootkas, Bella Coolas and other fishing peoples of the northwest Pacific coast. The Tlingits of Glacier Bay inhabited the outer coast around Lituya Bay and had summer fishing and seal hunting camps in Dundas and Taylor bays and along the lowlands of Point Gustavus.

They depended upon the sea and rivers for food and established trade routes into the Interior of Alaska, the Yukon, and the Rockies of British Columbia. Navigating cedar canoes through treacherous tides, they made war and traded as far as southern British Columbia.

The Tlingits lived in settled communities of considerable size, built large longhouses made of cedar and hemlock and displayed their individual wealth as a sign of social status. Blessed with a temperate climate, extensive trade routes and an abundance of food, the Tlingits were secure and prosperous. They developed an elaborate social system and a complex culture.

Their art, for example, was based on animals and mythological creatures. Carvings were usually animals that had been given human features with the overall proportions changed to suit the shape of the final product, such as a carved oar handle or dish. Mythological characters included the bear, otter and raven, who was said to possess many human characteristics and was the creator of all things.

Left—*A meadow near the Dundas River.*
Below—*A waterway through the Beardslee Islands. The islands are rising out of the bay at the rate of 4 centimeters a year, a foot in 8 years, a meter in 25.*

The Tlingits were also great storytellers and their legends were passed from generation to generation. One legend of the Hoonah Kwan people, the group that once inhabited Glacier Bay, concerns the tremendous ice fields that covered their hunting and fishing grounds. In former times, the legend says, the Hoonah Kwan people fished and hunted with great success around the Beardslee Islands. Then a young girl, Kahsteen, who was being kept in seclusion at the onset of puberty, called the glacier down from the north out of spite for being kept alone. The glacier responded, forcing the people to retreat from their homes and move southward toward the mouth of the bay.

When they found out that Kahsteen had called it, the tribe wanted to leave her behind so the glacier would no longer chase them. But Kahsteen was young and might bear many children, so a barren old woman, Shaw-whad-seet, took her place and the people moved to a protected place called Hoonah. Tlingits say that, although Shaw-whad-seet could not have human children, after the glacier covered her she could have ice children; these are the calved icebergs in the waters of Glacier Bay.

More than three decades after the Russians discovered Alaska, Glacier Bay was visited by the English Capt. James Cook, who made note of the range of peaks dominating

Ice is not just a winter feature, but an integral part of the environment at Glacier Bay. Below—*An iceberg, commonly seen.*

Left—*A somewhat animal-like natural ice sculpture seen at Goose Cove.*

Below—*The wicked devil's club,* Echinopax horridum (*"armed throughout with prickles"*), *is a tough, hardy species. It is here seen thriving in the dense shade of a spruce forest along the Dundas River.*

Mining

A mining company, active in exploration in the Monument for several years, has staked a large nickel deposit under the ice of Brady Icefield. They have used the west arm of Dundas Bay as a base, and put drilling rigs on the icecap, manned by a large crew and supplied by helicopters. It is rumored that the company's long-range plan is to develop a townsite at Dixon Harbor with access roads leading to the mine. Smelting would be done either at the townsite or in Gustavus.

Understandably in these times of environmental concern there has been conflict in this matter. Mining people, citing that they are within the law, claim they will be able to operate "out of sight, out of mind" in their remote location insofar as general public view is concerned. They say that careful planning and operation can permit mining with minimum degradation of the natural environment.

Those who disagree say human impact to a degree harmful to the environment would be inevitable, and that otter, bear, wolves and other animals that do not do well with man's encroachment will suffer.

Mining company base of operations on the west arm of Dundas Bay.

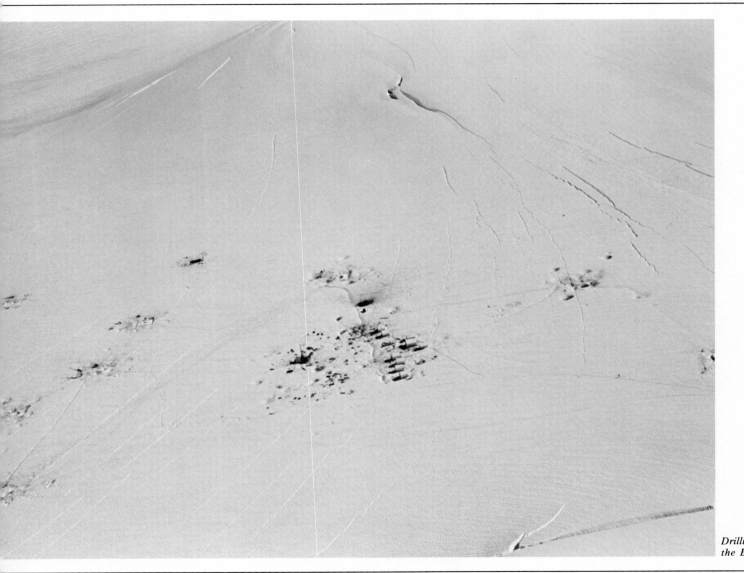

Drilling for nickel on the Brady Icefield.

Glacier Bay's coastline. He named the highest Mount Fairweather.

The French also became interested in the coastal waters of Southeastern Alaska. In 1786, Lituya Bay, on the Monument's outer coast, was discovered by Jean Francois La Perouse.

About 100 years later prospectors in search of gold swept through the Alaska Panhandle and into the Yukon. Prospectors were active on the outer coast, especially near

Opposite—Fairweather Glacier, in the northwest corner of the Monument. Mount Fairweather (15,300 feet) is the mountain mass to the left; Mount Salisbury (12,170 feet) is in the far right background. Above—Peaks east of Melbern Glacier, north of the Monument in Canada.

Lituya Bay. Many rusting ore tracks, steam engines and tools still litter the area, crumbling remnants of a brief era.

John Muir made the first of several visits to Glacier Bay in 1879. Scientist Harry Reid and the Reverend George Wright shared Muir's interest in the area and joined him at what is now called Muir Point to conduct scientific field studies. Glacier Bay's main ice field's rate of flow was determined by Reid and Wright, and Reid gathered enough data to later publish the first scientific study of Glacier Bay's natural history and geology.

In 1924, the federal government placed 4,000 square miles around Glacier Bay into temporary withdrawal status. A year later, the reserve was reduced to 1,820 square miles and Congress established Glacier Bay National Monument.

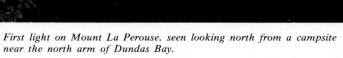
First light on Mount La Perouse, seen looking north from a campsite near the north arm of Dundas Bay.

Later, because of the continuing high interest of prospectors in the area, Congress passed a bill that would permit mineral exploration and development in the Monument; the law is still in force.

Dundas Bay and the eastern shoreline of Excursion Inlet were sites of salmon canneries and fish traps at the turn of the 20th century. The remains of old docks exist in both areas and, at Dundas Bay, a large oil tank, a cabin and a broken fish trap are all that remain of a once-large community.

Congress enlarged Glacier Bay in 1939 to its present size and the townsite of Gustavus voted to secede from Park Service lands. It remains outside today. Park Service headquarters were established at Bartlett Cove.

Above—*Sunset on the Red Mountain peaks.*
Right—*The sun drops behind the rim of the Brady Icefield.*

Plant Life

Glacier Bay's dramatic process of glacial recession creates conditions that bring a diversity of plant communities and life zones to the area. Where glacial fluctuations have occurred, plant diversity is seen, expressed in the process known as plant succession. Where glaciation has not disturbed the landscape, plant communities developed unhindered for several thousand years and became stratified into a series of life zones largely determined by altitude and moisture.

At sea level in the Monument, the moderate climatic conditions allow a temperate range of plant species that are also found in British Columbia and the State of Washington. The zone is a typical Pacific coastal rain forest where giant hemlock and spruce trees grow.

At about the 2,500-foot level, stunted and twisted forms of other, hardier trees and shrubs grope for existence in the subalpine zone. This zone also ranges from the heartland of Alaska south to the higher mountain ranges of California.

At still higher elevations, climatic conditions approach those on the treeless Arctic North Slope. The plant community at this elevation is made up of both arctic and alpine plant species. Broad slopes of alpine meadows reach up to the barren rock and ice-covered high mountains of the Monument.

The retreat of the ice mass that once covered the region altered the pattern of plant community development typically found elsewhere. In place of an altitudinal distribution of plant life zones, here one finds pioneer plants colonizing terrain recently bared by ice and building a soil layer which contains the nutrients necessary for less self-sufficient species. Over centuries, a succession of plant communities will flourish and die in a given area. In the lower elevations of the Monument, plant succession

56

Left—*A spruce forest and the Dundas River.*
Below—*A sundew plant; a shag mushroom.*

Opposite—*A place of quiet in Hugh Miller Inlet.*

57

culminates in the muskeg-hemlock rain forest, the highest level of plant development.

The relatively recent steady withdrawal of the Glacier Bay ice field left progressive examples of plant succession along the length of the fjord from the still-emerging spruce forests of Bartlett Cove to the barren escarpments of the Muir and Grand Pacific glaciers.

Several decades after the recession of a glacier, newly bared land begins to change from sterile moraines to a mosaic of pioneering plants. At first the soil is low in critical nutrients, but hardy species such as dwarf fireweed, dryas, horsetail and mosses and lichens are able to colonize areas that are stable and have sufficient moisture.

Alder seedlings and willows are found sparsely scattered among the pioneers. As the soil layer improves with a build-up of humus and nutrients, buffaloberry, an important food source for bears, and scrub willow begin to form thickets above the mats of dryas.

Opposite—*Dwarf fireweed on Sealer's Island.* Above, top to bottom, from left—*A wild garden in a bed of moss; bearberry; creeping willow colonizing on dryas mats; buffaloberry; moss borders the creek edge; lichens; a meadow of yellow dryas near Red Mountain; dryas mats at Geikie Inlet.*

Overleaf—*A field of wild flowers on the Dundas River.*

Top to bottom, from left—*Rusty menziesia, bog cranberry, twisted stalk, skunk cabbage, rhododendron.*

Alder forms an overstory of thick branches and leaves 40 to 60 years after the glacial retreat. Cottonwoods rise with the alders, and those that reach above the thicket canopy gain ample sunlight for growth and reproduction. They win only temporary dominance, however, as Sitka spruce begins to grow in the understory.

Spruce eventually dominates and forms a pure stand that excludes most light from the forest floor. A limited group of plants is able to survive in the increasingly dense shade. Plants that do proliferate include a variety of mosses, several species of fern, pink pyrola, rattlesnake plantain, early blueberry, goatsbeard and the shade-tolerant western hemlock. The forest of Bartlett Cove, only 200 years ago covered by ice, represents this stage of succession.

Western hemlock will eventually displace Sitka spruce except on mineral soils and along exposed beaches. Other tree species may share this dominance, depending upon the soil substrate and the level of the water table. Alaska yellow cedar and mountain hemlock compete with spruce at wet sites, such as the edges of bogs.

Bordering the mature beaches well above high tide and adjacent to the forest edge are fireweed, red elderberry, alder and devil's club. Many edible herbs grow near the high-tide mark. These include goosetongue, seashore plantain and Siberian spring beauty, along with scurvygrass and the tart sandwort.

Opposite—*Devil's club.*

64

Top to bottom, from left—*Yellow violet, western columbine, monkshood, buttercup, moss campion, bog orchid.*

65

Paintbrush. Nine species range over most of Alaska, and extend into Canada and Siberia.

Top, left to right—*Shooting star, fireweed, chocolate lily, Canadian dwarf dogwood.*
Bottom, left to right—*Mushroom, willow, silverweed, purple mountain saxifrage.*

Right—*Yellow warbler, a male.* Below—*Rock ptarmigan.*

Birds

The great variety of birds found in Glacier Bay National Monument is the product of both the Monument's wide range of habitats and its strategic location in the center of the Pacific flyway. Of the 206 bird species recorded in the Monument, however, only a few—about two dozen species—are permanent residents, hardy enough to survive and adapt to the long and cold winter months.

A great many Monument birds are temporary summer residents. They winter in southern latitudes and migrate north to nest. The birds can successfully rear young in the North during this time, since there's an abundance of seeds and insects to provide the great amount of protein needed during nesting. Since species of insects and seeds vary according to plant communities and successional stages, the birds that rely on them also vary, each species nesting and feeding in habitats where their preferred food source may be found.

In addition to the abundance of summer residents are the migrants that, for only brief periods during spring and fall, feed and rest on preferred habitats throughout the Monument. Because Glacier Bay is on the Pacific flyway—the westernmost route used by both migrating waterfowl and terrestrial birds—great concentrations of the birds may be seen during these times.

Opposite—A mature bald eagle. The bald eagle is found from the Aleutians to New Mexico, but is most numerous in coastal Alaska and British Columbia. It feeds principally on fish and carrion.

Below—Gull eggs blend so well with vegetation as to be almost unseen. These shells are apparently from eggs that have hatched. Bottom—A cormorant nest with three eggs. The cormorant's eggs are less well camouflaged than a gull's, but laid in more inaccessible places.

Young bald eagles—the downy pair about 6 weeks old and the fledged bird older. Eagles may lay up to three white eggs in the spring, which hatch by early June, but usually only one of the young survives through fledging. The first to hatch has a head start, and will either peck the younger chicks to death or force them out of the nest.

During the spring some of the migrants may remain to nest if they locate a suitable habitat. Many bound for the Arctic, for example, become attracted to the Monument's early successional stages of vegetation and settle to nest instead of continuing farther north. Such areas are characteristic of the upper and mid-regions of the bay, and consist of pioneer plant communities similar to the Arctic tundra and Aleutian grasslands of more northerly latitudes.

The coastal rain forest and muskeg and the intertidal plant communities attract many bird species usually associated with temperate zones. Most of these species also may be found throughout Southeastern Alaska and coastal British Columbia where these habitats occur, demonstrating their dependence upon a specific plant community or habitat type—although exceptions do occur. Certain species such as the hermit thrush, raven and bald eagle may range from areas of brushlands to the deep forest of the lower bay.

The greatest variety and concentrations of waterfowl and marine bird life may be found where their food source is readily available. These areas include the narrow passages of the Monument where tiderips and water turbulence mark the tide changes. Nesting of these birds occurs primarily at locations that are relatively safe from predators: islands and intertidal cliffs.

The localities that support the greatest variety of terrestrial birds are beaches, alpine meadows and brushlands, areas which have an edge effect, providing both cover and an abundant food source.

Red-necked grebe.

Common loon.

73

Above—*Semipalmated plover, gull eggs.*
Above right—*Willow ptarmigan.*
Right—*Kittiwakes and mew gulls.*

Birds that are found in habitats reflecting the pioneer stages of plant succession in the Monument include the snow bunting, the rock ptarmigan and the common redpoll. Mew gulls, semipalmated plovers, Arctic terns and killdeer found there also nest on the gravel soils of glacial outwash plains. Mew gulls, for example, bare only a small patch of dirt, lining the depression with a minimum of feathers for insulation of the eggs.

In the brushier localities of deglaciated terrain a greater bird diversity is found. This is the favored habitat of the willow ptarmigan, whose preferred food is the nutritious willow catkin. Also associated with this stage of succession are the pine grosbeak, whose thick bill is well adapted to crushing seeds, the small yellowish orange-crowned warbler and the hermit thrush. The orange-crowned warbler

migrates from as far south as Panama and Colombia during the spring to nest throughout the Pacific Northwest and Alaska. If spring is late, the bodies of many adults, dead of starvation, litter the beaches.

Geese are abundant along the tide flats, concentrated primarily in Adams Inlet, where they are protected by the Park Service. They molt during midsummer, seeking the shelter of the isolated islands in the center of the upper inlet.

Bird life in the more mature climax spruce-hemlock forest includes the blue grouse, winter wren, robin, hermit thrush, varied thrush, Oregon junco and raven. Ravens are notorious for their great variety of imitating calls and their cunning ability to steal food from other birds, even the young and eggs.

Above left—*Herring gull.* Above—*Semipalmated plover, Arctic tern, rock ptarmigan.*

Along the brushier regions adjacent to tidewater the yellow, myrtle and Wilson's warblers forage for insects along the intertidal zone at low tide. Robins and hermit thrushes feed higher in the adjacent brush thickets.

A bird that frequents the streams of the forest, the water ouzel, a medium-sized gray bird, is noted for a constant bobbing motion. It is most often seen meandering along the boulders of a clear stream, darting in and out of the water, searching for aquatic insects.

At the higher elevations and alpine regions of the Monument, the hardy gray-crowned rosy finch and the water pipit live. Pipits also are recognized by their bobbing antics, which easily give them away when they are walking on snowfields foraging for insects. The gray-crowned rosy finch frequents snowfields, too, feeding on a small segmented worm, the iceworm, that is found only on ice and perennial snow. The iceworm feeds on wind-deposited algae and pollen.

Top to bottom and left to right—*Lapland longspur, golden-crowned sparrow, myrtle warbler, Wilson's warbler, rufous hummingbird.*

Top to bottom and left to right—*Common murres, a kittiwake colony, pigeon guillemots, tufted puffins, a northern phalarope.*

Many summer resident birds associated with the sea congregate on islands, cliffs and sandy beaches to breed, near a concentrated source of food that is needed to feed both the nesting adults and the young. These feeding areas include the narrow passages that create tremendous tidal disturbance, and to a lesser extent, glacial fronts.

Marine bird life in the tidewater glacial systems of the upper regions of the bay include glaucous-winged, herring and mew gulls, kittiwakes and Arctic terns. Hundreds of gulls and terns are often seen wheeling and diving into the water, feeding.

A far greater abundance and variety of marine birds reside in the midsection and lower portions of the bay, areas that produce larger concentrations of food. Herring and glaucous-winged gulls, kittiwakes, pigeon guillemots, pelagic cormorants, murrelets, northern phalaropes, murres and horned and tufted puffins are some of the birds that use this almost unlimited supply of food.

Pelagic cormorants are found all along the Pacific rim from Japan to Mexico. They build nests of seaweed and grass on rock outcrops and in caves at the edge of the sea.

Above—*Yellowlegs and sandpiper, common shorebirds.*
Right—*Common goldeneye.*

Along the intertidal zones of the bay a variety of birds feed on the mussels, insects, marine worms and other invertebrates exposed by the falling tide. This bird population includes the long-legged and -beaked greater yellowlegs, sandpipers, surfbirds, the ruddy turnstones and the black oystercatcher.

The sheltered bays and intertidal channels of the Beardslee Islands are prime habitats for nesting ducks such as the goldeneye and common merganser. During fall and spring migration periods, other ducks are present, including oldsquaws and pintails.

Above—*Terns feeding off the face of Riggs Glacier.*
Left—*Black oystercatchers.*

81

Mammals

Mammals in the Monument are generally the same land and marine species that are common to most of Southeastern Alaska. Marine mammals are found throughout the salt-water regions of the area, where there are large concentrations of food and there is protection from predators. Land mammals, however, have a more limited distribution, because in many areas access is poor and food sources are nonexistent.

Like birds, mammals are generally dependent upon a specific habitat for survival. Relatively mobile species such as moose, bear, coyote and wolf may range as transients through barren or recently deglaciated areas that cannot support them from home bases in more favorable surroundings.

The mountain goat and red squirrel are examples of two nonpredator mammals that are dependent upon a certain spectrum of plants for their diet. Red squirrels, for example, stay in spruce forests because they depend primarily on spruce seeds for food. Mountain goats are closely associated with the alpine communities, where they forage on a variety of shrubs and herbs that grow there.

Predators, especially those that prey on a wide range of species, are not restricted to a habitat or successional vegetation type and their distribution covers a greater land

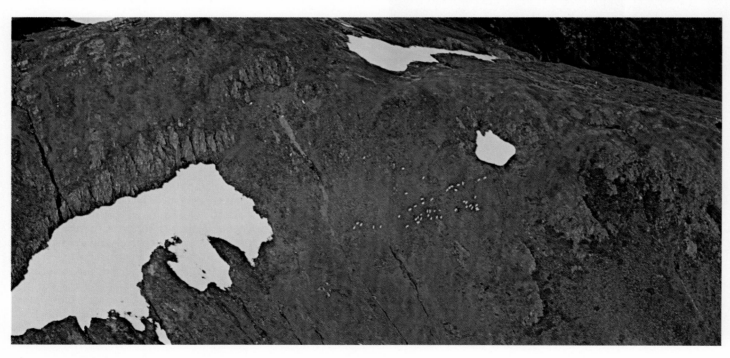

The mountain goat moves easily in his near-vertical world and is frequently seen by visitors to the Monument. The best goat groupings, however, are spotted from low-flying aircraft, as above.

Right—*River otter at Dundas Bay.*
Below left—*Hoary marmot, seen here in its dark phase.*
Below—*Pine marten.*

area. Wolves, coyotes and wolverines may be found in a wide variety of settings. Predators dependent upon a specific prey will be limited by the range of that species.

In the Glacier Bay area, the first mammals to colonize the pioneer stages of plant succession following deglaciation were small mammals—the deer mouse, wandering shrew, long-tailed vole and red-backed vole. These now inhabit a variety of mature plant communities. Voles, for instance, are most often found in beach grass bordering the shore.

An increase in the variety of small mammals develops in the more mature vegetational stages, especially where an edge effect occurs. The spruce-hemlock forest supports, for example, the red-backed vole, which makes its home in the litter of decayed trees and moss that covers the forest floor, the water shrew, northern flying squirrel and red squirrel. The water shrew inhabits fresh-water streams.

Mountain goats graze in the summer on alpine grasses and sedges, annual flowers, shrubs and lichens. In the winter they feed at lower elevations, favoring willow buds, dried grasses and even the buds of spruce. Often they have to paw through several feet of snow in order to reach any grass.

Opposite—The house and grounds of a red-backed vole. The vole may range over a quarter of an acre, constructing runways such as these as it goes.

Black bears come black, white, blue, cinnamon and brown, all color phases of the same species. Left—The glacier bear is the blue phase.

The swimming bear is a black.

Above—The first brown-phase bear recorded this far north was photographed by Captain Howard Robinson of Glacier Bay Yacht Tours. Right—Bear tracks at Fern Harbor.

They are specially equipped for their mode of diet, having long teeth (which become worn with age from constantly chewing dry and dusty plant material) and a ruminant's stomach. Bacteria in stomach compartments process the plant roughage by a series of steps that break down the plant tissues into usable protein.

These animals are not true goats but descendants of the old-world antelope tribe and are well adapted to rugged alpine life. Mountain goats are socially gregarious animals and form groups that are often segregated by sex.

Ranging over a greater variety of habitats than goats, three types of bear inhabit the Monument: the rare glacier

Foxes are common at lower elevations in the Monument.

Opposite—Black bear eating roots.

Left—*A harbor seal on the ice of Muir Inlet; a sea lion at South Marble Island; hair seals basking on a rock.*

bear (a color phase of the black bear), the black bear and, the largest of the group, the brown bear. Bears are omnivorous, eating both plants and animal flesh, and may become efficient predators when the opportunity arises.

The once-abundant sea otter has been brought to near extinction by the fur trade started by the Russians. In 1968, a small colony of animals was reintroduced to the rocky coastline, where the Steller sea lion is already abundant, but the attempt failed. River otter and mink, however, inhabit the salt-water bays and fresh-water rivers and streams.

Mammals of Glacier Bay's marine environment include harbor seals, porpoises and whales.

Harbor seals use the icebergs of the upper bay as spots for sunning and resting; more important, it is where females find protection while giving birth to their pups in the spring.

Below—*Harbor seals at Muir Inlet.* Right—*Hair seal caring for her pup.*

Dall porpoise (David Sykas).

Killer whales (center top and right), males much larger than females. Upper right—Humpback whale blowing.

Previous page—A humpback whale kicks for bottom.

Humpback whale broaching above.

Two other marine mammals common to the region's main channels, including Icy Strait, are Dall and harbor porpoises. Pods of harbor porpoise are especially abundant during the summer in the bays and inlets of lower Glacier Bay. Both species feed on small fish.

The euphausids and krill that support many fish in the bay also provide a rich food supply for other specialized feeders, the baleen whales of Glacier Bay. These large mammals cruise 25 to 150 feet below the surface, feeding on tremendous volumes of krill and small fishes by trapping in their baleens and moving this food on to their stomachs. The baleen is a series of long, bonelike curtains that forms a filtering device. Baleen whales common in the Monument include the humpback and minke whales.

The humpback, the most common whale in the Monument, is a stocky whale that grows to about 50 feet, black on top, white-bellied and white-throated. Its head is studded with rows of knobs. Its thickset body and its extremely long, irregularly edged flippers and large flukes help to identify it. It is one of the most active and playful of whales, for it likes to roll on the surface and it "lobs"—stands on its head and thrashes the

surface of the water with its flukes. It leaps frequently—one whale may leap 20 successive times.

This is the songster, famed for its various-pitched musical voice, which occasionally has been heard with the unaided ear by observers in boats, but which in recent years has been recorded with sophisticated electronics gear. Humpbacks are commonly observed during the summer months in the lower regions of the bay, in pods of up to 25. Their spouts can be seen and heard for at least half a mile.

The minke, or little piked, whale is the smallest of the baleen whales, rarely exceeding 33 feet in length. It is generally found close to the shore, where its small size and a broad white band across the fore flippers set it apart from other baleen whales.

A species of whales seen less frequently is the killer whale. A toothed whale, it is relatively small, the males seldom exceeding 30 feet, the females 25. The bold white-and-black color pattern is distinctive, as is the male's slender, several-foot-high dorsal fin cutting through the water, rising and falling as the blunt head breaks the surface.

Large fore flippers and flukes give the streamlined killer whale more speed than most whales. There are 20 to 28 sharp, interlocking teeth that can shear a porpoise or a seal in two—and destroy the largest whale.

Killer whales are usually seen in groups, or "packs," and attacks on prey are coordinated.

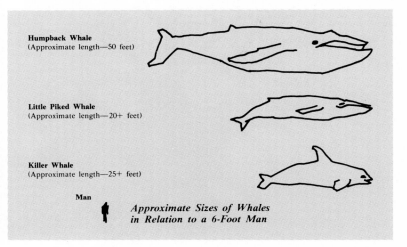

Humpback Whale
(Approximate length—50 feet)

Little Piked Whale
(Approximate length—20+ feet)

Killer Whale
(Approximate length—25+ feet)

Man

Approximate Sizes of Whales in Relation to a 6-Foot Man

Marine and
Fresh-Water Life

Because of the extensive fjord system and glacial watersheds, a broad range of marine and fresh-water habitats exist in Glacier Bay National Monument. Marine habitats vary in depth and salinity; they include deepwater channels, straits, fjords, bays, salt-water estuaries and tide flats. Fresh-water habitats vary according to the quality and temperature of the water and include rivers, streams, lakes and ponds, many of which have glacial sources.

The area's marine and fresh-water life forms are the product of the abundant food source that stems from a progressive chain found in both fresh water and salt water. Basic to the food chain are microscopic algae and phyto-plankton that thrive in the cold salt water from the Pacific Ocean. Their abundance, in turn, supports the next step in the ascending order of the food chain, zooplankton, and billions of invertebrates and crustaceans in their larval stages. A specialized segment of the crustacean group, krill, that belongs to the family *Euphausiidae*, is extremely abundant. It is food for baleen whales.

In the narrow passages of the lower bay, zooplankton is brought to the surface by the swift currents. Many species of small fish—herring, eulachon, sandlace and capelin, all averaging less than 10 inches in length—concentrate in large schools to feed. These fish become an important food

The great variety of intertidal life. Opposite, clockwise—Kelp, alaria, bloodstar, basket starfish. Right—Waterfall flows to the inlet. Evidence of the life present in a tidal inlet shows on the rock wall.

95

Left—*Coral and sponge.* Bottom left—*Red algae.*

Above—*Chitons are mollusks with eight plates or valves. They live attached to rocks or other surfaces. Most chitons, including the two shown here, are just a few inches long, but one species—the giant chiton—grows to 14 inches.*

osite—*Rockweed at Young Island.*

Near right—Urechis caupo, *a wormlike resident of the mudflats.* Far right—*A bristle worm, one of the polychaetes.*

Above—*Quarter-inch-long shrimp found in the water near an ice field, Tarr Inlet.* Right—*The crab boat* Adeline.

source for marine birds, porpoise and harbor seal, as well as for larger fish—halibut, cod, sculpin and salmon.

Crabs and shrimp also are important parts of the area's marine resources. Three species of crab are found in the Monument's waters: tanner, king and Dungeness.

During the summer the king crab is usually found in the deep water of the outer coastal shelf. In contrast, the Dungeness crab stays in shallower waters, migrating to deeper water during the winter. Dungeness are common

Mya truncata, *an uncommon bivalve with a distinctive spoon-and-socket hinge.*

A more than casual study of algae.

Sea urchin.

Above—*The tasty Dungeness crab.* Top right—*The author* (*right*) *needs some help to hold up the 65-pound halibut he caught.* Middle right—*Spawning sockeye salmon.* Right—*Ice in Goose Cove.*

around the Beardslee Islands, Bartlett Cove, Dundas and Taylor bays and Excursion Inlet. Tanners are found in the same waters as Dungeness and both may be gathered along the sandy intertidal beaches of Bartlett Cove during the spring neap tides.

Shrimp are prevalent in the bay, being most abundant at Charpentier Inlet and Goose Cove.

Halibut are important to the commercial and sport fisheries of the area. Halibut distribution includes the southmost waters of the Monument, Cross Sound, Icy Strait, Dundas and Taylor bays, and the midpart of Glacier Bay as far north as Goose Cove. The fish are found both in very shallow bays and in channels several hundred fathoms deep. They spawn during the winter at depths of 150 to 200 fathoms. Halibut eggs and larvae are carried by currents to shallow water where they begin to grow. When they are older, they move to deeper water where they can attain a weight of almost 500 pounds.

Five species of salmon are present in the salt- and fresh-water systems of the Monument: chum, pink, cohoe, chinook and sockeye. Their anadromous life cycle varies slightly according to species. Generally, it begins with adults migrating home from the open sea where they have matured to the fresh-water river or lake system where they hatched. The females choose a segment of stream where they create a redd (gravel depression) and lay their eggs, which are fertilized by an accompanying male and covered by a thin layer of gravel.

The survival of the eggs through the winter depends on climatic conditions. If, for example, the river system experiences flooding or heavy glacial siltation, the amount of oxygen available to the buried eggs is reduced and the embryos suffocate.

Eggs that survive the winter develop into hatchlings (alevin) that wriggle out of the gravel by spring. Depending on the species, the alevin may either head immediately to sea or remain in fresh water for a year or two before entering salt water. During this time they maybe eaten by yearlings of their own species, sculpin, trout, dragonfly nymphs or birds. The percentage of survival of those that do reach adulthood is low, about one to two percent. During the

Opposite—*The seiner* Horizon *at work off Southeastern Alaska* (*Howard Robinson*).

Below—*Adams Inlet and the Chilkat Mountains under clouds; sunrise at Geikie Inlet.* Right—*Algae and the intertidal life zone at Taylor Bay.* Below right—*Starfish eating a clam (inverted and held with pebbles for the photographer).* Bottom right—*Littleneck clams at Dundas Bay.*

earliest stages of their entrance into salt water, and while still in estuaries, the young swim together in enormous schools. As they grow in size, they move out to the vast reaches of the North Pacific to mature and again complete the life cycle when they return to fresh water.

The Dundas, Excursion, Bartlett, Beartrack and Salmon rivers and the rivers of the outer coast support most of the active salmon runs in the Monument. All are located in mature watersheds that have a consistent and relatively

pure water supply. Colonization of new rivers by salmon is generally rapid. The Bartlett River, for example, was created by the retreating Glacier Bay ice field less than 160 years ago, and it now supports large fall runs of cohoes, reds and pinks.

Progressively unfavorable conditions for salmon survival are found up the bay where new glacial rivers emerge. Still, stray salmon may attempt to spawn in these rivers. Pinks have been found as far glacierward as Nunatak Cove of upper Muir Inlet, indicating some possibility of successful spawning in glacial rivers such as those that enter Geikie, Charpentier and Adams inlets.

Other species of fish in the salmonid family native to the Monument are steelhead, which spawn and live in the rivers of the outer coast, cutthroat, and the Dolly Varden trout.

Left—Shag Cove in Geikie Inlet, Tlingit Peak (3,274 feet) in background. Center—Geikie Inlet, looking southwest toward Wood Lake. Above—Intertidal algae zonation shows on the rock wall of Taylor Bay.

Hikes and Cruises

Glacier Bay National Monument's varied scenery can be enjoyed by the experienced hiker, small boat handler or excursion boat passenger. Those who plan to hike or climb in the Monument should register with the National Park Headquarters at Bartlett Cove.

Transportation into the Monument is primarily by air. Alaska Airlines has daily flights from Juneau to Gustavus, the small community adjacent to the southern border of the Monument. Boats or planes can also be chartered and private boating arrangements are possible.

A 12-mile gravel road connects the National Park Headquarters at Bartlett Cove with Gustavus; scheduled buses transport visitors between the two. Bartlett Cove has campsites, plus overnight accommodations at the facilities of the licensed concessionaire, the Glacier Bay Lodge Company. Reservations are necessary. The lodge also sells marine gas and diesel fuel and operates a 9-hour boat tour to the head of the bay. The tour boat will drop off and pick up hikers at points en route for a small additional fee. Glacier Bay Airways offers scenic flights and transportation for backpackers to many areas of the Monument.

For those who intend to hike overnight, several items are essential: a good down sleeping bag, wool socks, a change of clothing (down clothing is lightest, but wool is far warmer when wet) and mosquito repellent. Raingear should be sufficiently durable for hiking thorugh wet brush. Rubber boots that reach 12 inches above the ankle will keep the feet drier than other forms of footwear. A backpack stove is necessary for cooking in the upper regions of the Monument because wood is not available.

The following hikes and boat trips are recommended:

BARTLETT COVE

Home base for traveling around the Monument. An interpretive trail winds through a 200-year-old stand of spruce and hemlock that is interspersed with small ponds, remnants of the Glacier Bay ice field of the 1700's. Beaches and coves are within easy walking distance. At low tide, the intertidal mud flats give access to the good clamming and crabbing on many of the adjacent islands. Sea birds are abundant and bald eagles frequent the area. Humpback whales often come into the cove during summer months, spending several days within view of the lodge.

From the dock at night one can see photoluminescent zooplankton glowing brilliantly when disturbed by a paddle swirled through the water, evidence of the water's rich nutrient content.

Author William Boehm above Muir Glacier.

BARTLETT RIVER AND LAKE

Reached by a trail from National Park Headquarters through several miles of spruce and hemlock forests. Mosquitoes can be extremely bad during the spring and early summer. Cutthroat trout in the lake strike wet flies.

Opposite—*Spruce forest near Bartlett Cove.*

EXCURSION INLET

A fjord system at the southeast edge of the Monument, 2 hours by boat from Bartlett Cove. The east arm of the inlet ends in an extensive tidal marsh at the outlet of the Excursion River. Fishing is fair for cutthroat.

ADAMS INLET

Left to right—The shoreline of Adams Inlet; moss-covered spruce on North Marble Island; fog-shrouded mountains of the Chilkat Range rise from Adams and Excursion inlets.

Several hours north of Bartlett Cove by tour boat. A canoe or kayak is needed for transportation to Adams from Muir Inlet (aircraft are banned from the area to protect nesting geese). This shallow salt-water basin—the product of an outwash plain dumped by the Casement and Adams glaciers—offers excellent views of the Chilkat Range and Endicott Gap. There is clear walking along the extreme eastern end of the inlet, heavy brush only around the Klotz Hills on the inlet's northern shore.

Top—*Sunrise on Mount Wright.*
Bottom—*Muir Inlet from Mount
Wright.* Opposite—*Sunset on the
Fairweathers. An unsurpassed
view of the entire bay area,
sunrise to sunset, is had from
Mount Wright.*

108

MOUNT WRIGHT

Approximately 25 miles north of Bartlett Cove, and the most recommended and accessible viewpoint in the Monument. The overnight trip involves a moderate to strenuous steep hike, beginning a few hundred yards south of Muir Point. The tour boat will let off hikers anywhere in this vicinity. The easiest hiking terrain is a steep ridge that rises just south of the point and avoids the younger brush stands. Several hours of scrambling through alternating rocky open ledges and brush patches leads to dwarf willow and alpine meadows that begin at the 1,800-foot level. Scores of mountain goats graze above. Campsites are abundant at about 3,500 feet, along the rolling ridges at the base of Mount Wright. A view of the entire bay area includes Muir Inlet, Casement Glacier, Adams Inlet, Glacier Bay and the Fairweather Range. Ptarmigan and the gray-crowned rosy finch are numerous, and small ponds and streams are abundant in the upper reaches of the meadows.

Geese and a yellowlegs in Goose Cove, and icebergs on the beach.

GOOSE COVE

On the east shore of Muir Inlet 35 to 40 miles north of Bartlett Cove; access by tour boat. A hike that requires only a few hours begins along the beach south of the cove, reaching a large cut-wash canyon where Forest Creek flows into the bay from Casement Glacier.

An overnight trip to Red Mountain is more demanding. A trail leads up along a small creek starting 100 yards south of the Park Service tent, through some alder and into the meadows. An alternative starting point is Nunatak Cove, heading due east across dryas-covered moraines, then northeast to the brush-covered lower slopes of the peak. Two to four hours of navigating through brush reaches an alpine plant-covered ridge that leads to the top of 3,600-foot Red Mountain. Camping is outstanding near several clear, small lakes near the top of the ridge, where there is a view of most of the bay and the Fairweathers. There are many goats in the high-country scenery.

Climbing the ridge to the top of Red Mountain rewards the hiker with views of Muir Inlet and most of Glacier Bay, the Fairweathers and clear alpine lakes.

Three scenes at White Thunder Ridge. The bottom photo is a view through Glacier Pass to Mount Fairweather.

WHITE THUNDER RIDGE

Approximately 40 miles north of Bartlett Cove, along the west shore of Muir Inlet; access by tour boat. A hiking trail starts from the north end of Wolf Cove, opposite the edge of McBride Glacier across the inlet. There is sufficient shelter for private boats but double anchoring is recommended to offset the force of tide changes.

A small river that drains the receding and stagnant ice fields of the basin northwest of the ridge leads about three-quarters of a mile through alternating brush and open dryas-covered slopes; hikers then turn northeast along the ridge to fairly open rocky terrain that is beginning to become vegetated. Alder thickets occur primarily along the creek drainages and can be avoided during the several hours it takes to reach the ridge. Toward the clearing at the top, many small, clear lakes are bordered with rock, alpine flowers and dwarf willow. Excellent swimming, campsites and a view of the Fairweathers and the upper peaks of Muir Inlet.

MUIR GLACIER

About 50 miles north of Bartlett Cove, 4 to 5 hours by tour boat. Moderate glacier travel and rock scrambling along the northwestern trim line of the glacier (ice ax and rope teamwork needed) offer a close-up view of moraines, crevasses and the forces at work in a glacier system.

Muir Glacier is a remnant of a 4,000-foot-thick ice field that covered the bay's exterior forests 2,100 years ago. It began its recession from the mouth of Muir Inlet at the turn of this century.

113

Hugh Miller Inlet; Gilbert Island.

HUGH MILLER INLET

About 35 miles northwest of Bartlett Cove, southeast of Gilbert Island. The island is connected at low tide to the mainland at its northern shore, where a small passage of salt water existed 25 to 35 years ago, but retreating glaciers have allowed the land to rise. Now the passage is almost entirely above high tide.

At the entrance to the inlet, a few small rocky islands are exposed at low tide, but the main body, to the north and south, is deep. Charpentier Inlet to the south is deep and narrow. Day hikes from its head lead to outwash canyons with unique formations.

From midpoint in Hugh Miller Inlet, Mount La Perouse can be seen above the lower peaks that rise through Hugh Miller Glacier. Classic U-shaped valleys lie in the Scidmore and Hugh Miller drainages. Anchorage is excellent at the northern end of the inlet. An enjoyable 2-day hike to the northern ridge circling the Scidmore glacial basin requires some mountaineering experience and the use of an ice ax. Along the beach just north of the river draining the glacial system, the way heads west toward the northern foothills and till of the ridge to be climbed, through dryas-covered moraines and occasional scattered alder, but no brush, to the base of the ridge. A scramble up through broken shale and till gains the top of the 900-foot knob. From here it is necessary to traverse the melting snowfields to reach the southwest of the ridge and the steep heather slopes beneath. Exposure to the basin below occurs for only 100 feet and is safe. If this stretch is covered with snow, an ice ax is recommended. (An alternative route north of the snowfield heads up a steep shale and rock talus incline to meadows.)

Beyond the snowfield, a basin faces the Scidmore Glacier. Further climbing leads to a ridge of alpine meadows at about 2,800 feet and the base of the rocky ridge that connects with the summit. It is possible to reach the peak by simple rock scrambling without a rope. A long, gentle slope drops to the west and Brady Icefield below, offering many campsites with snow and water. The views from the summit include the Fairweathers, Tarr Inlet and the southern portions of the bay.

Above, middle—*Scidmore Peak and ice bowl below.*
Above—*Hugh Miller Inlet and Glacier. This cove is calle(d) Wierd Bay by some, but the name is not official and not universally recognized.*

Left—*The Brady Icefield in the background behind Hugh Miller Glacier.* Below—*A hiker contemplates Scidmore Peak.*

Top—*July Fourth Mountain.*
Bottom—*The south tongue of Geikie Glacier at Abyss Lake outlet.*

116

Left—*The south tongue of Geikie Glacier, a small lake and the headwaters of the Dundas River.* Below—*July Fourth Mountain and Geikie Inlet.*

GEIKIE INLET

Easily navigable, about 2½ to 3 hours (25 miles) west of Bartlett Cove. On the northern shore, anchorage is best at its upper end. A day hike leads to the northern tongue of the Geikie Glacier and the base of July Fourth Mountain. An overnight trip can be taken to Lake Seclusion and Wood Lake. The first part of the trip is brushy; about half-way, spruce and hemlock forests make travel easier.

Clockwise—*Abyss Lake; source of the Dundas River; spring runoff running beneath the ice.*

DUNDAS BAY

About 20 miles due west of Bartlett Cove, a little more than 1½ hours at moderate speed by boat. Dundas provides an interesting variety of habitats to explore. In certain portions of the bay, notably the north arm, only canoeing is allowed. A Park Service cabin on the west shore near the mouth of the bay is used by two park rangers. On the east shore, opposite the cabin, lie the rich meadows of the Dundas River.

Up-to-date charts are needed to reach the west arm of Dundas Bay. A shallow shoal of rocks just off a clump of islands at the junction of the north and west arms may create a hazard. The west arm has many anchorages if overnight hiking is planned; double anchorage provides the most security.

An interesting 3-day hike, requiring an ice ax and minimal mountaineering experience, originates from the head of the north arm at a muskeg adjacent to the western shore. A waterfall lies northwest less than half a mile away at about the 1,200-foot level, up forested slopes cut by avalanche chutes choked with snow and brush. The falls and the basin's outlet can be reached within 3 hours. The boulder-strewn meadow that supplies the falls leads to a alpine ridge at about the 2,000-foot level, the goal for the first day. Northwest of the

Clockwise—*Peaks at 3,700 feet; old timbers rotting back into the earth; muskeg at Dundas Bay.*

abundant campsites is a three-peaked ridge whose snowfields yield scores of waterfalls that drop over a 1,000-foot cliff to a basin below. That ridge is the second day's goal. Visible beyond it in the distance is Mount La Perouse.

A clear lake at the northern base of the first saddle is the beginning of the climb up a steep, brushy slope that quickly yields to a gradual heather- and alpine flower-covered ridge. This ridge leads to the three-peaked ridge and more campsites. The ridge, averaging 3,100 feet in elevation, affords a sweeping view of the Fairweathers to the west and the Brady Icefield below.

Due north along the snowfield at the head of the basin, a steep granite drop-off faces north toward the river draining Abyss Lake. On the east side of the horseshoe basin's ridge, a steep snow chute descends to the river and must be negotiated by careful glissading. Beyond the upper portion of the chute, it's easy going all the way to the bottom and there is no extreme exposure. Due east, the river joins the silt-laden outlet of the southern tongue of the Geikie Glacier. With other streams, they become the Dundas at Dundas Falls. South of the falls, about 50 yards upstream, lies a smaller lake, then a small ridge followed by another small ridge covered with mountain hemlock. The final few miles to the head of the bay, completing the loop, are through a forested valley and lake system that feeds the north arm of Dundas Bay.

Top—*Fern Harbor.* Bottom—*We fly down a three-peaked ridge north of Dundas Bay.*

Top—*At the source of the Dundas River.* Bottom—*Abyss Lake outlet.*

Opposite—*Dundas Falls, at the source of the Dundas River.*

Epilogue

I was greeted by a cold, wet and gloomy June day on my first visit to Glacier Bay. After carrying all my backpacking and camera gear off the Twin Otter that had just flown us through a typical "southeaster" rainstorm, I waited in a light drizzle at the Gustavus airstrip for a National Park Service pickup. Occasionally through the heavy mists I caught brief glimpses of a nearby muskeg covered with snow and patches of spruce. This was to be my first season as a park ranger, my third trip to Alaska.

The first week was spent at Bartlett Cove, Park Headquarters for the Monument, reconditioning the three patrol boats to be used for the summer. Chuck Janda, chief ranger, briefed us on our duties and conduct as rangers and reviewed for us the principles of marine navigation. It was a rainy week and everyone patiently hoped for a clear day that would reveal the surrounding mountain ranges.

The Fairweathers were still hidden by heavy mists and clouds the following week when we moved to our summer

Opposite—*Fog takes over Excursion Inlet.* Above—*Mount Fairweather.*
Right—*Fog is no stranger to a fisherman.*

base of operations at Dundas Bay. It didn't matter; there was far too much to experience and see close at hand. Wildlife was amazingly abundant, especially seals and marine birds. Bald eagles were beginning to nest, and other birds that had just arrived from tropical wintering grounds were beginning to sing the territorial songs.

Our home turned out to be an old, dilapidated cannery shack. We quickly made it presentable but it continued to let in just enough mosquitoes through the cracks to keep us swatting at night. The cabin was set on deteriorating pilings parallel to the shore, and the whole structure wobbled when someone walked across the floor.

Clockwise—*Moss and rocks at Wachusett Inlet; a stream at Dundas shows glacial debris on the bottom; Graves Harbor; Dixon Harbor.*

Opposite—*A stream at Wolf Point.*

A cold fresh-water stream emerged from the hemlock forest only a few feet from the cabin and supplied us with plenty of water. Its outlet emptied into a small cove facing the cabin entrance, a great source of cutthroat trout, halibut and Dungeness crab.

The view from Dundas was incredibly beautiful on the day that the Fairweather Range finally cleared, two weeks after my arrival at the Monument. The icy crags of Mount La Perouse and Mount Crillon rose dramatically above the

Above—The author's cabin on Dundas Bay. Top right—Sunset on the Alaska-Yukon border. Right—Fog clearing on Dundas Bay.

Opposite—On the left is Mount Bertha (10,204 feet). The dominant peak on the skyline is Mount Crillon (12,726 feet).

ove, top to bottom from left—*Lichen, mountain heath, columbine,
splash of a waterfall, the author on the Brady Icefield.*

posite—*Tarr Inlet near Scidmore Peak.*

green-forested foothills of Dundas Bay. This day marked the real beginning of my fever to explore and to learn what I could of this great wilderness that had unfolded before me, and I thought of the completeness of God's creation manifested in such ruggedness and beauty.

During the summer I began to comprehend how immense and varied Glacier Bay is, and what a unique experience it offers. Through my own experiences, and from watching the reactions of new visitors to the Monument who had never seen a mountain, fjord, or whale, I became more aware of what a wilderness experience means, especially during this age of encroaching civilization.

In Glacier Bay you can explore the bays, fjords and rocky coastline by boat, leaving only the disappearing wake of the motor as your imprint on the environment. You can also share today the experience of the Tlingits canoeing through fog-shrouded fjords and wilderness coves, or walk through carpets of mountain avens and alpine meadows that have never before felt the footprint of man.

This exhilation that is shared when viewing a sunset breaking through the clouds and storms of the Fairweathers after a hard day's climb, watching a wolf family teaching its pups how to hunt for mice and feeling the warm sun piercing the cold dampness of a foggy morning are only a small part of my memories of Glacier Bay. With this publication I hope to share Glacier Bay's wealth in natural history, and its value as a wilderness resource.

—*William D. Boehm*

Opposite—*The sun goes west from the Monument's outer boundary at Sea Otter Creek.*

Glossary of Plants and Animals

PLANTS

Alder—*Alnus crispa*
Asphodel—*Tofieldia glutinosa*
Avens, broad-leaved—*Geum macrophyllum*
Azalea, alpine—*Loiseleuria procumbens*
Azalea, false—*Menziesia ferruginea*
Bearberry—*Arctostaphylos uva-ursi*
Blueberry, alpine—*Vaccinium uliginosum*
Blueberry, early—*Vaccinium ovalifolium*
Buffaloberry—*Shepherdia canadensis*
Buttercup—*Ranunculus* sp.
Cedar, Alaska yellow—*Chamaecyparis nootkatensis*
Columbine—*Aquilegia formosa*
Copper flower—*Cladothamus pyrolaeflorus*
Crowberry—*Empetrum nigrum*
Currants—*Ribes* sp.
Deer cabbage—*Fauria crista-galli*
Deerberry—*Maianthemum dilitatum*
Devil's club—*Oplopanax horridus*
Dogwood—*Cornus canadensis*
Dryas—*Dryas drummondii*
Elderberry, red—*Sambucus racemosa*
Fireweed—*Epilobium angustifolium*
Fireweed, dwarf—*Epilobium latifolium*
Fleabanes—*Erigeron* sp.
Gentian—*Gentiana* sp.
Geranium—*Geranium erianthum*
Goatsbeard—*Aruncus sylvester*
Goldthread—*Coptis asplenifolia*
Goosetongue—*Plantago maritima*
Harebell, mountain—*Campanula lasiocarpa*
Heather—*Phyllodoce* and *Cassiope* sp.
Hemlock, mountain—*Tsuga mertensiana*
Hemlock, western—*Tsuga heterophylla*
Horsetails—*Equisetum* sp.
Huckleberry, red—*Vaccinium parvifolium*
Labrador tea—*Ledum palustre*
Luetkea—*Luetkea pectinata*
Lupine—*Lupinus* sp.
Marigold, marsh—*Caltha palustris*

Monkshood—*Aconitum delphinifolium*
Paintbrush—*Castilleja* sp.
Plantain, rattlesnake—*Goodyera oblongifolia*
Plantain, seashore—*Plantago macrocarpa*
Pyrola, pink—*Pyrola asarifolia*
Rhododendron, alpine—*Rhododendron lapponicum*
Salmonberry—*Rubus spectabilis*
Sandwort—*Honckenya peploides*
Saxifrages—*Saxifraga* sp.
Scurvygrass—*Cochlearia officinalis*
Skunk cabbage—*Lysichiton americanum*
Spring beauty, Siberian—*Claytonia siberica*
Spruce, Sitka—*Picea sitchensis*
Sundews—*Drosera* sp.
Twisted stalks—*Streptopus* sp.
Violet, bog—*Pinguicula vulgaris*
Water lilies—*Nymphaea* and *Nuphar* sp.
Willows—*Salix* sp.

ANIMALS

Birds

Bunting, snow—*Plectrophenax nivalis*
Chickadee, chestnut-backed—*Parus rufescens*
Cormorant, pelagic—*Phalacrocorax pelagicus*
Crow, northwestern—*Corvus caurinus*
Eagle, bald—*Haliaeetus leucocephalus*
Finch, gray-crowned rosy—*Leucosticte tephrocotis*
Flycatcher, western—*Empidonax difficilis*
Goldeneye, Barrow's—*Bucephala islandica*
Goose, Canada—*Branta canadensis*
Grosbeak, pine—*Pinicola enucleator*
Grouse, blue—*Dendragapus obscurus*
Guillemot, pigeon—*Cepphus columba*
Gull, glaucous-winged—*Larus glaucescens*
Gull, herring—*Larus argentatus*
Gull, mew—*Larus canus*
Hummingbird, rufous—*Selasphorus rufus*
Junco, Oregon—*Junco oreganus*
Killdeer—*Charadrius vociferus*
Kinglet, golden-crowned—*Regulus satrapa*

Kinglet, ruby-crowned—*Regulus calendula*
Kittiwake, black-legged—*Rissa tridactyla*
Loon, red-throated—*Gavia stellata*
Mallard—*Anas platyrhynchos*
Merganser, common—*Mergus merganser*
Murre, common—*Uria aalge*
Murrelet, marbled—*Brachyramphus marmoratum*
Oldsquaw—*Clangula hyemalis*
Ouzel, water—*Cinclus mexicanus*
Oystercatcher, black—*Haematopus bachmani*
Phalarope, northern—*Lobipes lobatus*
Pintail—*Anas acuta*
Pipit, water—*Anthus spinoletta*
Plover, semipalmated—*Charadrinus semipalmatus*
Ptarmigan, rock—*Lagopus mutus*
Ptarmigan, willow—*Lagopus lagopus*
Puffin, horned—*Fratercula corniculata*
Puffin, tufted—*Lunda cirrhata*
Raven—*Corvus corax*
Redpoll, common—*Acanthus flammea*
Robin—*Turdus migratorius*
Sandpiper, least—*Erolia minutilla*
Sandpiper, rock—*Erolia ptilocnemis*
Sandpiper, spotted—*Actitis macularia*
Scoter, surf—*Melanitta perspicillata*
Scoter, white-winged—*Melanitta deglandi*
Siskin, pine—*Spinus pinus*
Sparrow, fox—*Passerella iliaca*
Sparrow, Lincoln's—*Melospiza lincolnii*
Sparrow, savannah—*Passerculus sandwichensis*
Sparrow, song—*Melospiza melodia*
Surfbird—*Aphriza virgata*
Swallow, barn—*Hirundo rustica*
Swallow, tree—*Iridoprocne bicolor*
Tern, arctic—*Sterna paradisaea*
Thrush, hermit—*Hylocichla guttata*
Thrush, Swainson's—*Hylocichla ustulata*
Thrush, varied—*Ixoreus naevius*
Turnstone, ruddy—*Arenaria interpres*
Warbler, myrtle—*Dendroica caronata*
Warbler, orange-crowned—*Vermivora celata*
Warbler, Townsend's—*Dendroica townsendi*
Warbler, Wilson's—*Wilsonia pusilla*

Opposite—A stream dropping to the bay at Tidal Inlet in the Monument's center.

Warbler, yellow—*Dendroica petechia*
Waxwing, Bohemian—*Bombycilla garrula*
Wren, winter—*Troglodytes troglodytes*
Yellowlegs, greater—*Totanus melanoleucus*

Fish

Halibut—*Hippoglossus stenolepis*
Salmon, chum (dog)—*Oncorhynchus keta*
Salmon, king (chinook)—*Oncorhynchus tshawytscha*
Salmon, pink (humpback)—*Oncorhynchus gorbuscha*
Salmon, red (sockeye)—*Oncorhynchus nerka*
Salmon, silver (cohoe)—*Oncorhynchus kisutch*
Steelhead—*Salmo gairdneri*
Trout, cutthroat—*Salmo clarki*
Trout, Dolly Varden—*Salvelinus malma*

Salmonid Species for rivers of Glacier Bay

Bartlett River—red, cohoe, pink, cutthroat, Dolly Varden
Berg River—red, cohoe, cutthroat, rainbow/steelhead, Dolly Varden
Dundas River—red, dog, pink, cutthroat, Dolly Varden
Excursion River—dog, pink, cohoe, cutthroat, Dolly Varden
Outer coast—cohoe, dog, rainbow/steelhead, Dolly Varden

Mammals

Bats—*Myotis* sp.
Bear, black—*Ursus americanus*
Bear, brown—*Ursus arctos*
Coyote—*Canis latrans*
Deer, blacktail—*Odocoileus hemionus*
Fox, red—*Vulpus vulpes*
Goat, mountain—*Oreamnos americanus*
Hare, varying—*Lepus americanus*
Lynx—*Lynx canadensis*
Marmot, hoary—*Marmota caligata*
Marten, pine—*Martes americana*
Mink—*Mustela vison*
Moose—*Alces alces*
Mouse, meadow jumping—*Zapus hudsonius*
Otter, river—*Lutra canadensis*
Otter, sea—*Enhydra lutris*
Porcupine—*Erethizon dorsatum*
Porpoise, Dall—*Phocoenoides dalli*
Porpoise, harbor—*Phocoena phocoena*
Sea lion—*Eumetopias jubata*
Seal, harbor—*Phoca vitulina*
Seal, northern fur—*Callorhinus ursinus*
Shrew, Glacier Bay water—*Sorex alaskanus*
Shrew, masked—*Sorex cinereus*
Shrew, wandering—*Sorex vagrans*
Squirrel, northern flying—*Glaucomys sabrinus*
Squirrel, red—*Tamiasciurus hudsonicus*
Vole, long-tailed—*Microtus longicaudus*
Vole, tundra—*Microtus oeconomus*
Vole, tundra red-backed—*Clethrionomys rutilus*
Weasel, least—*Mustela rixosa*
Weasel, short-tailed—*Mustela erminea*
Whale, humpback—*Megaptera novaeangliae*
Whale, killer—*Orcinus orca*
Whale, minke—*Balaenoptera acutorostrata*
Wolf—*Canis lupus*
Wolverine—*Gulo gulo*

Other

Crab, Dungeness—*Cancer magister*
Crab, king—*Paralithodes camtschatica*
Crab, tanner—*Chionocetes* sp.
Iceworm—*Mesenehytraeus solifugus*
Krill—*Euphausia* sp.
Shrimp—*Pandalus* and *Pandalopsis* sp.